Walking with the Women of the New Testament
Study Guide
(Volume 1)

Written by Heather Farrell
Designed by Heidi Hillman

For more study helps visit womeninthescriptures.com

How to Use this Study Guide

I am thrilled that you have picked up this study guide, as it means that you are intending to undertake your own personal study of the women of the New Testament. I can testify that this is a journey that will change your heart and possibly your life. I know that as I have studied the women of the New Testament not only have I gained a greater understanding of myself, and my role as a woman in God's Kingdom, but I have also come to better understand Jesus and who he was. This is a journey that I would love to assist in making a very special and meaningful one for you. Ideally this study guide is to be used in conjunction with my book, "*Walking with the Women of the New Testament*", but of course you are free to use it in whatever way suits you. I should also specify that I use the King James Version of the Bible and that all my scripture references are taken from that translation. I also assume that you are using the version of the scriptures published by The Church of Jesus Christ of Latter-day Saints. If you are not you can find the Topical Guide and Bible Dictionary I often refer to in this Study Guide here https://www.lds.org/scriptures/study-helps.

With that said, let's get going!

Step 1 -- Print off and organize your Study Guide

If you have the professionally bound copy of this Study Guide then you are ready to go, but if you have the PDF version of this Study Guide you will want to first print it off and then either have it spiral bound or three-hole-punch it and put it in a binder. Either way is fine. The benefit of a binder is that it makes it easy to add in additional pages to each women's study section. On the other hand, the benefit of having it bound is that you won't have to worry about pages getting lost or torn out.

As you go through this study guide you will see study prompts that ask you to use the additional pages found in the back of your study guide-- like the character study, timeline, etc. To use these pages simply photocopy the page from the back of the book and then paste or tape the page into the woman's section you are studying. That way you keep all of your study materials and thoughts about each women organized and easy to find for future reference. It might be helpful to make some photocopies of the additional study pages before you begin your study so you will have them ready for easy access when you need them. Feel free to add in talks, quotes, images or any other study helps you find that enrich your study of the New Testament. Also, you will want to print off the bookmark that is included in the back of the study guide which you will want to photocopy onto cardstock and use it as you go through your study.

Don't worry about getting through the New Testament quickly. Going slowly and really studying these women's lives in depth will be so much more meaningful to you than seeing how quickly you can progress through the books. It might take you three months to complete this study guide, or three years, but either way it will be an incredible journey… so don't rush it.

Step 2--Open up your New Testament and start reading in Matthew.

I have listed the women in the Study Guide as they appear in the New Testament. I only included REAL women, who lived and breathed during the time of the New Testament. This means that you won't find the women in parables, Jesus's teachings or women from the Old Testament (with the exception of the women in Christ's lineage) in this Study Guide. I have left a blank study template in the back of the Study Guide that you can photocopy and add in other women you want to study.

Step 3-- Stop when you find a woman in your reading and take time to understand her story.

I have included a bookmark with this study guide that has questions you can ask yourself each time you come across a new woman. Take the time to think about these questions and record your thoughts in the study guide page dedicated to her. If you need help with this process, or would like to go more in-depth I have included questions and study suggestions in the Study Guide for each woman (or set of women) that will help you dig deeper into their stories and help you find personal application.

At the end of your study guide you will also find additional study pages that will assist you with your study. These pages include:

Character sketch

Use this page to study a character from the scriptures more in-depth. Write their name (or a draw a picture) in the center square and then make a list or a "cloud" of all the attributes, virtues and character traits you see in them as you study. This page can also be used to do a topical study on a word, like "virtue" or "compassion".

Timeline

Use this page to create timelines of events in the New Testament. Don't be too concerned with getting dates right, you just want to get an idea of what order the events happened. Using the "Harmony of the Gospels" or the Bible Chronology in the Bible Dictionary of the LDS Version of the Scriptures may also be helpful.

Storyboard

Use this page to draw (or write) out a story from the New Testament. This can be a visual way to keep track of people, places and events.

Compare and Contrast

There are three different compare and contrast sheets. Choose which one to use depending on how many different accounts there are of the story in the New Testament. For example, you'd want to use the one with four spaces for the story of the Damsel and Maid at the Door because it is told in all four Gospels., but you'd want to use the one with three for the story of the Daughter of Jarius because it is only told in three of the Gospels.

Maps

I have included blank maps of the New Testament Bible lands for you to mark and fill in. Using maps can be a very valuable tool in increasing your understanding of the history and people of the

New Testament. Use the Bible Maps in the the appendix of your LDS version of the Bible (or see them here https://www.lds.org/scriptures/bible-maps) to help you fill them in.

Step 4- Open Up "*Walking With the Women of the New Testament*"

After you have spent time studying the woman for yourself and formed your own ideas about her, then I hope you'd open up my book, "*Walking with the Women of the New Testament*" and read what I have to say about her. You may also find some of my thoughts on my blog, Women in the Scriptures (http://www.womeninthescriptures.com) Don't worry if what I say and what you say don't match up. The beauty of studying the scriptures is that the stories can be interpreted in many different ways—there is no wrong and there is no right way to look at it. Let the Holy Ghost teach you and lead your study and you will learn what YOU need to know. Enjoy what others have to say and their insights, but trust yourself and what the Holy Ghost teaches you.

Step 5-- Share what you have learned about the women of the New Testament with someone else.

I promise that as you delve into your scriptures looking for the women you will find a treasure trove of wisdom and will gain powerful personal revelation. Don't hesitate to share this with others. Trust me the world needs more people sharing the amazing stories of the women in the scriptures. So open your mouth and bear your testimony about what you have learned.

That's it!

You are ready to begin your walk with the women of the New Testament, but before you begin let me leave you with one final thought. In a wonderful talk Elder Dallin H. Oaks gave in January of 1995, entitled "Scripture Reading and Revelation" he said:

"The word of the Lord in the scriptures is like a lamp to guide our feet (seePs. 119:105), and revelation is like a mighty force that increases the lamp's illumination manyfold…Just as continuing revelation enlarges and illuminates the scriptures, so also a study of the scriptures enables men and women to receive revelations. Elder Bruce R. McConkie said, "I sometimes think that one of the best-kept secrets of the kingdom is that the scriptures open the door to the receipt of revelation" . This happens because scripture reading puts us in tune with the Spirit of the Lord." … We do not overstate the point when we say that the scriptures can be a Urim and Thummim to assist each of us to receive personal revelation."

I know what Elder Oaks said is true. The scriptures are the gateway to revelation, and if we want a deeper understanding of our purpose here on the earth, direction in our lives, answers to hard questions and solutions to problems we will find those answers as we commune with the Lord through scripture study.

I hope that as you undertake this journey with the women of the New Testament that you will learn more about your divine mission on this earth. I hope that you will feel of God's incredible love for all of His daughters and feel of His love of you. Most of all, I hope that you will come to better know Jesus Christ and let him change your heart and your life.

Additional Resources to Use in your Study

You will notice as you progress through this Study Guide that in the "Ideas for Additional Study" I will often refer you to other sources. These sources aren't necessary, the Holy Ghost can teach you most everything you need to know, but they can be very useful for better understanding the history, language and people of the New Testament.

1826 Webster's Dictionary

This is one of the oldest English dictionaries and is now available online, as an iPad App, and in printed book form. This dictionary is a valuable resource in your study, especially if you are using the King James version of the Bible. The meaning and usage of many words has changed over the last hundred years, and sometimes our understanding of scriptural passages can be hindered because we are giving a modern meaning to a word whose older meaning is quite different. The 1826 Webster's Dictionary can be found online at http://1828.mshaffer.com/

Strong's Concordance

Strong's Concordance was first published 1890 and is basically an index to the Bible. It allows readers to find the original Hebrew or Greek words that are used in the Bible and to compare how the same word is used in other places in the Bible. It isn't a translation of the Bible but is meant to be used by people who don't read Hebrew or Greek in order to help them gain a more accurate understanding of the Bible.

Strong's Concordance was originally printed in book form and you can still buy and use it that way. They also have concordances that are online and which I have found are much faster and easier to use. My favorite concordance is one I found at a website called Bible Study Tools (http://www.biblestudytools.com/). I have the website saved to my ipad and when I study my scriptures I often pull up the website to check the original meaning of words that seem confusing or out of place to me. The concordance is really a wonderful tool if you want to delve deeper into your scriptures.

If you would like more instructions on how to use one I have a post on my blog, Women in the Scriptures, that explains how to use an online version (http://www.womeninthescriptures.com/2013/07/how-to-use-strongs-concordance-to.html). If you have access to a paper concordance the process is pretty much the same, just more page flipping.

Look at a Different Translation

Sometimes it can be helpful to look at a different translation of the Bible to understand the meaning of a passage. Not only does this sometimes help clarify the language of a passage but I also shows you other ways in which the same words can be translated, giving you a deeper understanding of the passage. If you normally use the King James Version of the Bible you may want to refer to a newer translation and if you normally use a new translation you might want to refer to the King James . It is amazing how looking at the same words from a different perspective can help illuminate their meaning. Personally I like to use a website called Bible Study tools (http://www.biblestudytools.com/) because under "Bible Study" they have a tool called "Compare Translations". This tool allows you to type in any verse in the Bible and see several different translations of the same verse.

Use the Online Scriptures

The Church of Jesus Christ of Latter-day Saints has a wonderful online search tool for the scriptures. It can be found at https://www.lds.org/scriptures. Several times in this Study Guide I will encourage you to look up words or phrases on this website using the "search" bar on the right hand side. The online scriptures can be a fast and easy way to find other ways in which a word, or similar phrase, is used elsewhere in the scriptures. It can also help you connect scriptures together in ways that you might not have thought of before. It can also just be a fast way to find a scripture that you can't remember the reference for!

The COMPLETE Joseph Smith Translation of the Bible

If you are using the LDS version of the Bible you will notice that often throughout the bible there will be footnotes with the abbreviation "JST". This refers to the "Joseph Smith Translation" and indicates that they are passages where Joseph Smith was instructed by God to clarify the meaning of the scriptures. These JST footnotes are extremely helpful in understanding the meaning of certain passages and give much needed insight. Sometimes you will see a footnote that refers you to the Appendix of the Bible where longer translations are included.

It is also important to note that not ALL of the corrections that Joseph Smith made to the Bible are included in the footnotes or the appendix of the LDS Scriptures. To see a COMPLETE listing of all of Joseph Smith's translations you must look at the full Joseph Smith Translation of the Bible (also called Joseph Smith's Inspired Translation of the Bible) which has been published by the Community of Christ. This translation has been available for many years but it has only been in the last decade that the Community of Christ allowed LDS scholars to view the original manuscripts. They found that the versions of Joseph Smith's Inspired Translation of the Bible, which had already been published by the Community of Christ, were true to Joseph Smith's original corrections. There is now a version of the full Joseph Smith Translation of the Bible compiled by BYU scholars and published by Deseret Book that allows you to view the original manuscript and make a side-by-side comparison of it to the KJV (it can be found at http://www.amazon.com/Complete-Joseph-Smith-Translation-Testament/dp/1590384393)

Maps

In the Appendix of the LDS version of the Bible there are several wonderful maps of the New Testament Bible lands. These maps are a wonderful resource and I'd encourage you to look up places that you read about as you study. It is amazing how understanding the geography and location of a woman's story can illuminate and clarify her experience. Using the maps can also help you make connections between other people and events.

Christ's Lineage

Scripture references:

Matthew 1
Luke 3:23-38

Words I looked up:

What I know about them:

Questions I have about them:

My thoughts about the women of Christ's lineage:

Additional scriptures I studied:

Ideas for additional study:

• Compare and contrast the lineage that is given in Matthew 1 and in Luke 3: 23-38. Why do you think both Matthew and Luke included Christ's family history in their accounts?

• Find and mark the five women that Matthew lists in the lineage of Christ. Take time to study each of these women. Ask yourself what role they played in Christ's family history and what is similar (and different) about each of their stories. Why would Matthew have included them in his history? You may want to do a character sketch on each of them:
    * "Thamar" or Tamar (Genesis 38)
    * "Rachab" or Rahab (Joshua 2)
    * Ruth (Ruth 1-4)
    * "her that hath been the wife of Uriah" or Bathsheba (2 Samuel 11)

Mary

Scripture references:

Matt 1:16, 18-25
Matt 2-11, 13-14, 20-21
Matt 12:46-50
Matt 13:55
Mark 3: 31-35
Mark 6:3
Luke 1:26-56
Luke 2:5-8, 16, 19, 22, 27, 34-35, 43-51
Luke 8: 19-20
John 2:1-5, 12; 6:42
John 19:25-27
Acts 1:14
Gal 4:4

Words I looked up:

What I know about her:

Questions I have about her:

My thoughts about Mary:

Additional scriptures I studied:

Ideas for additional study:

• Read through the verses about Mary and create a character sketch of her. What values did she exemplify through out her life?

• How many times does Mary "ponder" things in her heart? What do you think this means?

• Compare and Contrast Mary's Psalm in Luke 1 with Hannah's Psalm in 1 Samuel. How are these two women similar? How are they different?

• Create a timeline of Christ's life. As you do make sure to mark all the major events of Mary's life and search for evidence about how Christ felt about his mother and how she influenced his life and ministry. Using the "Harmony of the Gospels" found in the Bible Dictionary under "Gospels, Harmony of" (pages 684-696) should be helpful for this.

• Mary is the only woman in the scriptures whose name was known before her birth. Look up her name in the Index at the end of your triple combination and study what the Book of Mormon teaches about her.

• The name "Mary" is the Greek form of the name "Miriam" who was the sister of Moses. Look up "Miriam" in the Bible Dictionary (page 733) and study her story. As you read Miriam's story look for similarities and differences between her and Mary. Why might it be significant that they share the same name?

Peter's Mother-in-Law

Scripture references:

Matt 8:14-15
Mark 1:30-31
Luke 4:38-39

Words I looked up:

What I know about her:

Questions I have about her:

16

My thoughts about Peter's mother-in-law:

Additional scriptures I studied:

Ideas for additional study:

• Compare and contrast the accounts given in Matthew, Mark, and Luke. Why do you think her story was included in all three gospels?

• How do you imagine that this experienced influenced Peter's faith?

• What did she do after she was healed? What can you learn from her example?

Daughter of Jairus

Scripture references:
Matt 9: 18-19, 23-26
Mark 5: 22-24, 35-43
Luke 8:41, 49-56

Words I looked up:

What I know about her:

Questions I have about her:

My thoughts on the Daughter of Jairus:

Additional scriptures I studied:

Ideas for additional study:

• List all the women mentioned in this story. What do you know about each of them?

• Who demonstrated faith in this story? How?

• What possible significance do you see in the fact that the daughter of Jarius, whom Christ raised from the dead was 12 years-old (around the age when girls start menstruation) and that this woman who was healed by Jesus had been suffering with her " issue of blood" for 12 years?

• Compare and contrast the stories in Matthew, Mark and Luke. Why do you think this story is included in all three gospels?

Woman with an Issue of Blood

Scripture references:

Matt 9: 20-22
Mark 5:25-34
Luke 8:43-48

Words I looked up:

What I know about her:

Questions I have about her:

My thoughts on the Woman with Issue of Blood:

Additional scriptures I studied:

Ideas for additional study:

• What is different in the way that Jarius approached Jesus and the way in which this woman approached him? What times in your life have you been like Jairus? What times in your life have you been like the woman with the issue of blood?

• Study Leviticus 12, in which the Mosaic rules concerning menstruation are laid out. What was required of women? What was required of men? What would both of have experienced while a woman was menstruating? How would these rules have applied to a woman who had been bleeding for 12 years?

• Look up the word that is translated as "unclean" in the Strongs Concordance. Study the other scriptures listed with it. What other ways is this word used?

• Do a topic study on the word "virtue". Look it up in the 1828 Webster's dictionary, Strongs Concordance and study the references to "virtue" listed in the Topical Guide. Based on what you learn write your own definition of "virtue". How does what you learned change your understanding of what it means to be "virtuous"?

• How did Christ heal her physically? How did he heal her spiritually? Which do you think happened first?

Jesus's Sisters

Scripture references:

Matt 13:56
Mark 6:3

Words I looked up:

What I know about them:

Questions I have about them:

My thoughts on Jesus's Sisters:

Additional scriptures I studied:

Ideas for additional study:

• Make a list of all of Mary's children (see Matt. 1:25, Mark 6:3). What type of mother do you imagine her to be?

• Think about your own siblings and family. How have they influenced who you are? How would Christ's siblings and family have influenced who he was?

• Ponder on what you know of Christ's interactions and treatment of women. How might his sisters have taught him and helped him to understand women's feelings and viewpoints?

Herodias and Her daughter

Scripture references:

Matt. 14: 1-11
Mark 6:17-28;
Luke 3:19-20

Words I looked up:

What I know about them:

Questions I have about them:

My thoughts on Herodias and her daughter:

Additional scriptures I studied:

Ideas for additional study:

• Compare and contrast the accounts in Matthew, Mark and Luke. What details do you learn about her story from these accounts?

• Study the "Herodian Family Tree" on page 217 of "Walking with the Women of the New Testament" and Herodias' place on it. It may be helpful to re-draw this diagram into your study journal.

• Do a character sketch of her. What can she teach you about what NOT to do?

• Why type of influence did she have on her daughter? What was good about their relationship? What was bad about it? What can you take from their story that will help you improve your relationship with your mother? With your daughter?

• What messages is your example teaching the Young Women in your life? What are you doing well? What could you improve upon?

Women and children among the 4,000 and 5,000

Scripture references:

Matt 14:21
Matt 15:38

Words I looked up:

What I know about them:

Questions I have about them:

My thoughts on the Women and children among the 4,000 and 5,000:

Additional scriptures I studied:

Ideas for additional study:

• Draw a picture in your study guide of how many loaves and fishes each group started out with and how many each group ended up with in the end. What impresses you about these stories?

• What possible symbolism do you see in these stories?

• Study the sermon on the "bread of life" (John 6) and ponder on why Jesus would compare himself to bread. How does that relate to the story of the 4,000 and 5,000?

• What had just happened in Christ's life before the feeding of the 5,000? (see Matthew 14) How does this change your understanding of this story?

Syrophenician woman and her Young daughter

Scripture references:

Matt 15:21-28
Mark 7:24-30

Words I looked up:

What I know about them:

Questions I have about them:

My thoughts on the Syrophenician woman and her young daughter:

Additional scriptures I studied:

Ideas for additional study:

- What is the context in which this story is told? Why do you think Christ did not grant her request?

- Read the parable of the widow and the judge in Luke 18: 1-9. How does this parable relate to this woman's story?

- How does Christ say her daughter was healed?

- What can she teach you about faith? How might her faith have been similar to that of the Brother of Jared (see Ether 3)?

- Compare and contrast the accounts of her story in Mark and Matthew.

Mother of Zebedee's children

Scripture references:

Matt 20:20-23

Matt 27:56

Words I looked up:

What I know about her:

Questions I have about her:

My thoughts on the Mother of Zebedee's children:

Additional scriptures I studied:

Ideas for additional study:

• Compare and contrast the accounts of her approaching Jesus given in Matthew and Mark. What do you think she really wanted? What was Jesus was trying to teach her?

• Her sons were the apostles James and John. Study their lives by looking them up in Bible Dictionary ("James" is listed first on page 709 and "John" is on page 715). What type of men were they? What can you learn about her from their stories?

• Look up "Zebedee" in the Bible Dictionary (page 791) and study the references. What else can you learn about her from these scriptures?

• Why do you think she is only known to us as "the mother of Zebedee's children"? What does that title tell you about her and how may have been perceived by others?

• Some Bible scholars believe that she is the same woman as Salome (see page 145 in "Walking with the Women in the New Testament") . You may want to study these two women together and decide if you think that they are the same woman or different ones. The study page for Salome is on page 53 of this study guide.

Damsel and Maid at the Door

Scripture references:

Matt 26:69, 71
Mark 14:66- 70
John 18: 17
Luke 22:56-57

Words I looked up:

What I know about them:

Questions I have about them:

My thoughts on the Damsel and the Maid at the Door:

Additional scriptures I studied:

Ideas for additional study:

• Use the compare and contrast sheets to compare all four accounts of the denial. What is the same and what is different about each of them?

• What do you think Peter's reasons were for denying Christ? It may help to look up "Peter" in the Bible Dictionary and study the scriptures listed for him. Make a character sketch of him. What about his denial is in keeping with his character? What is not? You might also find the talk "Peter, my Brother" by Spencer W. Kimball a good resource to use as well.

• How would you react if you had been them and heard Peter deny Christ three times?

• Study John 12 and study how Christ reacted to Peter's denial. How many times did he ask Peter if he loved him?

• Have you ever been betrayed by someone you loved and trusted? How did you feel?

Additional scriptures I studied:

Ideas for additional study:

• Draw a timeline of Christ's trial, being sure to mark her involvement in it. Using the "Harmony of the Gospels" found in the Bible Dictionary under "Gospels, Harmony of" (pages 684-696) should be helpful for this.

• How do you think her message influenced Pilate's decision? What do you think she saw in her dream?

• Make a list of other people in the scriptures can you think of who were taught by God through their dreams. Look up their stories in scriptures. If you have a hard time thinking of people to study look up "Dreams" in the Bible Dictionary or "Dream" in the Topical guide for ideas of who to study.

• Think about some of the significant dreams that you remember and how they made you feel. If you haven't written about them in your journal take the time to do so and record your thoughts and feelings about them.

• Make a list of all the ways in which God speaks to you. How do you recognize his voice? Which ways are the loudest? Which ways do you need to pay more attention to?

Mary Magdalene

Scripture references:

Matt 27:57, 61
Matt 28:1-10
Mark 15: 40-41, 47
Mark 16: 1-8, 9-11
Luke 8:2-3
Luke 24: 1-11, 22-24
John 19:25
John 20: 1-3, 11-18

Words I looked up:

What I know about her:

Questions I have about her:

My thoughts about Mary Magdalene:

Additional scriptures I studied:

Ideas for additional study:

- What three events is she specifically mentioned in? What does her presence at these events tell you about her relationship with Jesus?

- Find Magdala on the map. What towns and cities are nearby?

- Study the references to "Sprits, Evil or Unclean" in the Topical Guide and make note of the different types of influences and what effects they have on people. What do you think it means that Mary Magdalene was healed of "seven devils"?

- Christ promised his disciples that those who followed him would have the power to cast out devils (Mark 16:17). As you study this topic notice ways in which righteous people exert power or influence over these spirits. In which ways, can you too "cast out" or over power evil influences in your life?

- Study John 20 in which Christ appears to her at the empty tomb. What can this interaction tell you about their relationship? Why do you think that Jesus appeared to her first and that she was the first to know that he was resurrected?

Mary, the mother of James and Joses

Scripture references:

Matt 27:56, 61
Matt 28:1-10
Mark 15: 40-41, 47
Mark 16: 1-8
Luke 24: 1-11, 22-24

Words I looked up:

What I know about her:

Questions I have about her:

My thoughts about Mary, the mother of James and Joses:

Additional scriptures I studied:

Ideas for additional study:

• What other name does this Mary go by? See Matthew 28:1 or "The Mary's in the New Testament" on page 79 of "*Walking with the Women of the New Testament.*"

• Make a list of the events she was present for. What can her presense at these events tell you about her?

• Study the lives of her sons James, the lesser and Joses (see entry #4 for "James" in the Bible Dictionary). What can you learn about her from her sons?

• Why do you think that Christ appeared to women first after his resurrection? Why do you think they were the first ones to touch him and to bear witness of him to others?

• Why do you think she and the other women at the tomb were not believed when they bore testimony of the resurrection?

The Widow who Gave Two Mites

Scripture references:

Mark 12:41-44
Luke 21:1-4

Words I looked up:

What I know about her:

Questions I have about her:

My thoughts about The Widow who Gave Two Mites:

Additional scriptures I studied:

Ideas for additional study:

• Where was Jesus teaching when he saw her? Why is this location significant to her story? You may want to refer to the diagram of Herod's Temple on page 129 of "Walking with the Women of the New Testament."

• How old do you imagine her to be? How does it change it your perspective of this story to imagine her as a young widow with children, a middle aged woman, or an old woman?

• Study "Money" in the Bible Dictionary (page 733) drawing pictures of the different types of money used during this time period. How much did this woman give? What do you think it would it be equivalent to today?

• Read the story of the rich young man in Luke Mark 10: 17-30. How is his story similar to this woman's? How is it different? Who do you most identify with the widow who gave her mites or the rich young man?

Salome

Scripture references:

Mark 15: 40-41
Mark 16: 1-8

Words I looked up:

What I know about her:

Questions I have about her:

My thoughts about Salome:

Additional scriptures I studied:

Ideas for additional study:

• What events is she present at? What other women that you have studied would also have been at these events?

• Why might some readers assume that she is the same woman as the mother of Zebedee's children?

• Read her story on page 145 of "*Walking with the Women of the New Testament*" and write down something new you learned or an additional question you have about her.

Scripture references:

Luke 1:5-80

Words I looked up:

What I know about her:

Questions I have about her:

My thoughts about Elisabeth:

Additional scriptures I studied:

Ideas for additional study:

• What was Elisabeth's lineage? What was Zacharias' lineage? What do you think is significant about their family heritage?

• Do a character sketch of Elisabeth. What qualities did she exemplify? Why would God have sent Mary to her before the birth of Jesus?

• Study the life of John the Baptist (for a list of scriptures to study see "John, the Baptist" in the Bible Dictionary.) What can you learn about her from his life?

• What do you think it means that John was "filled with the Holy Ghost" from his mother's womb? What type of influence would she have had in his life?

• Elisabeth told Mary "blessed is she that believed" what do you think she meant by that. How might that it apply to both Mary and Elisabeth?

• Elisabeth is the Greek version of the name Elisheba (see Exodus 6:23) who was the wife of Aaron, the brother of Moses. What possible significance to do you see that these two women had the same name?

Anna

Scripture references:

Luke 2: 36-38

Words I looked up:

What I know about her:

Questions I have about her:

My thoughts about Anna:

Additional scriptures I studied:

Ideas for additional study:

- Why was Anna privileged to see the Messiah?

- Do a character sketch for Anna. What qualities does she exemplify?

- Anna is among the few women in the scriptures called a "prophetess". Study the stories of the other women who are called "prophetesses" -- Miriam (Exodus 15:20), Deborah (Judges 4-5), and Huldah (2 Chronicles 34:32 and 2 Kings 22:14) – and notice what qualities they have in common. Why might Anna be included among these women? What did she do that made her a "prophetess"?

- It might also be interesting to study the women who are false prophetesses—Noadiah (Neh. 6:4) and Jezebel (Rev 2:20; 1 Kgs. 18:4, 13, 19; 19:1–2; see also 21:5–25; 2 Kgs. 9), and compare and contrast them to righteous prophetesses.

- Who do you think are our modern day prophetesses? How can you be a prophetess?

Widow of Nain

Scripture references:

Luke 7: 11-17

Words I looked up:

What I know about her:

Questions I have about her:

My thoughts about the Widow of Nain:

Additional scriptures I studied:

Ideas for additional study:

- Locate Nain on a map. What cities are close to it?

- What can you learn about Jewish burial customs from this story?

- Think about a woman you know who is a widow. What type of challenges does she face? How might those challenges be similar to what this woman experienced?

- Study the word "compassion" by looking it up in the Topical Guide. What do you think it means that Christ "had compassion" on this woman?

- What can this story tell you about how God feels about women?

Joanna

Scripture references:

Luke 8:2-3
Luke 24: 1-11, 22-24

Words I looked up:

What I know about her:

Questions I have about her:

My thoughts about Joanna:

Additional scriptures I studied:

Ideas for additional study:

• She is among the women who "ministered" to Jesus of her substance. What do you think that means? In what ways might she and other women have cared for or supported Jesus.

• Study the word "minister" and ponder on the different ways in which this word is used. You may want to look up the word in this verse that is translated as "minister" in the Strongs Concordance, study the listings for "minister" in the Topical Guide, and see "ministry" in the Bible Dictionary.

• What is it that Christ healed her of? How might her life have been different after she was healed? What challenges might she have faced before and after her healing?

• As a member of the Herodian household what influence do you think her healing may have had on Judea's leaders?

Sinner who washed Jesus' feet with her hair

Scripture references:

Luke 7:36-50

Words I looked up:

What I know about her:

Questions I have about her:

My thoughts about the Sinner who washed Jesus' feet with her hair:

Additional scriptures I studied:

Ideas for additional study:

• This story is very similar to that of the story told in Mathew 26, Mark14 and John 12. Read these stories and compare and contrast them with this account in Luke.

• When did this event take place in Christ's ministry?

• Do you think this woman was the same woman who anointed Christ's before his death? Why or why not?

Susanna and the Unnamed Women who Followed Christ

Scripture references:
Luke 8:2-3
Luke 23: 27, 49, 55
Mark 15:40-41
Matt. 27:55-56
John 19:25

Words I looked up:

What I know about them:

Questions I have about them:

My thoughts about Susanna and the Unnamed Women who Followed Christ:

Additional scriptures I studied:

Ideas for additional study:

• Study the scriptures about the women who followed Jesus (see Luke 8:2-3; 23: 27, 49, 55; Mark 15:40-41; Matt. 27:55-56; John 19:25). What impresses you about these women?

• Make a list of all the women you find who followed or ministered to Jesus. What do these women have in common? What is different about them?

• How do you imagine that these women "ministered" to Christ? What can you learn from their examples?

Martha

Scripture references:

Luke 10: 37-42

John 11: 1-6, 17-27, 34-45

John 12:2

Words I looked up:

What I know about her:

Questions I have about her:

My thoughts about Martha:

Additional scriptures I studied:

Ideas for additional study:

• Do a character sketch of Martha? What qualities does she exemplify? How is she different/ similar than her sister Mary?

• What events is Martha present at? What do you notice about her involvement?

• The parable of the good Samaritan is given right before we are first introduced to Martha (Luke 10: 30-37). Read through the parable but imagine that instead of a man the Samaritan is a woman (change the pronouns to feminine ones). How does reading the parable this way change your understanding of it?

• Why do you think that Jesus "tarried" when he knew that Lazarus was dying and Martha and Mary had asked him to come? Does God ever" tarry" in your life when you ask for help? Why might he do that?

Mary of Bethany

Scripture references:

Luke 10: 37-42
John 11: 1-5, 17-20, 28-34, 39-45
John 12:3-9

Words I looked up:

What I know about her:

Questions I have about her:

My thoughts about Mary of Bethany:

Additional scriptures I studied:

Ideas for additional study:

• Do a character sketch of Mary. What qualities does she exemplify? Create a picture in your mind of her. What type of woman do you see?

• What did Mary "choose" when Christ said that she "hath chosen that good part, which shall not be taken away from her" (Luke 10:42)?

• Study ALL of Luke chapter 10. Make a list of the events that happen and what instructions Christ gives. Why do you think that the story of Mary and Martha is included in this chapter?

• Compare and contrast the accounts of Mary anoininting Christ in Matthew, Mark and John. Why do you think Christ stated that what she did should be remembered for all generations?

• Study about anointing and why it was done. Use the Bible Dictionary ("anoint" on page 609) or the Topical Guide to find scriptures to study. Why might Mary have anointed Christ?

Certain Woman of the Company

Scripture references:

Luke 11:27-28

Words I looked up:

What I know about her:

Questions I have about her:

My thoughts about the Certain Woman of the Company:

Additional scriptures I studied:

Ideas for additional study:

- What is the context in which this story happens?

- What do you think prompted this woman's exclamation? Why do you think she stated that Mary's womb and breasts were blessed?

- Why do you think Jesus responded to her question like he did? What was he trying to teach?

- Read this story in the complete Joseph Smith Translation. What changes do you notice? How might this change the meaning of Christ's response to her?

Woman with a Spirit of Infirmity

Scripture references:

Luke 13:11-16

Words I looked up:

What I know about her:

Questions I have about her:

My thoughts about the Woman with a Spirit of Infirmity:

Additional scriptures I studied:

Ideas for additional study:

- Where did Jesus see this woman? Why do you think he noticed her?

- Have you ever struggled with your health? How did it affect your spirituality? How might this woman's infirmity have affected her physically and spiritually?

- What do you think it means that "Satan hath bound" her? How might that have been the root cause of her infirmity?

- How did Jesus heal her? How was it similar to how we give healing blessings today? How was it different?

- What did Jesus rebuke the Jews for? What does his response tell you about how he feels about women?

Daughters of Jerusalem

Scripture references:

Luke 23:27-31

Words I looked up:

What I know about them:

Questions I have about them:

My thoughts about the Daughters of Jerusalem:

Additional scriptures I studied:

Ideas for additional study:

• Study the account of Jesus triumphal entry in Matthew 21, Mark 11, and John 12. It might help to draw a picture of the events that happened. Where are the women in this event? What other things in this story are referred to as female?

• How many days before his crucifixion did the triumphal entry happen? You might want to create a time line of all the events that occurred between the time that he entered Jerusalem for Passover and then left it carrying his cross to Golgotha. Using the chapter headings and the "Harmony of the Gospels" in the Bible Dictionary will help you with this.

• Compare and contrast Jesus's triumphal entry to his departure from Jerusalem (account starts in Luke 23:26).

• What do you think that Jesus was trying to tell women in Luke 23:27-28? Why might have felt compelled to say what he said? Be sure to study the cross references and JST for Luke 23:31.

Women at the Empty Tomb

Scripture references:

Luke 24: 1-11, 22-24
Matthew 28:1-11
Mark 16:1-13
John 20: 1-18

Words I looked up:

What I know about them:

Questions I have about them:

My thoughts about the Women at the Empty Tomb:

Additional scriptures I studied:

Ideas for additional study:

• See page 151 in "*Walking with the Women of the New Testament*" and study the chart of the women who were present at the tomb. Read each account and draw a picture of each woman who there and what you know about her.

• Compare and contrast all four accounts of the women at the tomb (Matthew 28, Mark 16, Luke 24, John 20) what is the same about them, what is different? It may also help to create a timeline of the events you read about in these chapters and who was present at each event.

• What motivated these women to come to the tomb? What did they experience before and after?

• How were their testimonies received by others? How do you think this made them feel? Have you ever had someone doubt your testimony?

Samaritan Woman at the Well

Scripture references:

John 4: 7-42

Words I looked up:

What I know about her:

Questions I have about her:

My thoughts about the Samaritan Woman at the Well:

Additional scriptures I studied:

Ideas for additional study:

• Wells are a common theme throughout the Old and New Testament. What other women can you think of that had significant interactions at a well? If you need help thinking of women you might go to the online scriptures and type "well" or "well drink" into the search bar and study the references it pull up.

• Look up "Samaritan" in the Bible Dictionary (see page 768) and make a list of what you know about them. It might also help to make a list comparing what the Jews believed and what the Samaritans believed and highlight their main differences. You also might want to refer to "Samaritans" on page 165 of "Walking with the Women in the New Testament".

• Do a character sketch of this woman. How does she exemplify what Jesus taught in Matthew 5:6 and 3 Nephi 12:6?

• In D&C 4:4 it repeats a phrase used by Jesus in this woman's story (John 4:35). What phrase is it and why might the Lord have referred to this woman's story in this section? What was he trying to teach?

Woman Taken in Adultery

Scripture references:

John 8:1-11

Words I looked up:

What I know about her:

Questions I have about her:

My thoughts about the Woman Taken in Adultery:

Additional scriptures I studied:

Ideas for additional study:

- Where was Jesus when this woman was brought in to him? What is important about this location?

- Imagine for a moment that you were this woman. What would you have experienced? What would you have felt? How would you have wanted to be treated?

- Imagine that you are one of the people in the crowd around Jesus and this woman. What would you have experienced? What would you have felt? How do you think you would have reacted?

- You may want to read this story in the full version of the Joseph Smith Translation and identify what this woman did after her interaction with Jesus. How might her life have been different after this experience?

- Who do you relate to in this story? Why?

Mother of the Man Born Blind

Scripture references:

John 9:2-3, 18-23

Words I looked up:

What I know about her:

Questions I have about her:

My thoughts about the Mother of the Man Born Blind:

Additional scriptures I studied:

Ideas for additional study:

• Study the story of the man born blind in John 9. Why did Christ heal him? How did he heal him?

• Who believed him when he testified that Jesus had healed him?

• How did this man's parents react to his healing? Why do you think they reacted this way?

• How might this story relate to having our "spiritual eyes" opened?

Women at the Cross

Scripture references:

John 19:25
Mark 15:40-41
Matthew 27: 55-56

Words I looked up:

What I know about them:

Questions I have about them:

My thoughts about the Women at the Cross:

Additional scriptures I studied:

Ideas for additional study:

• Study John 19:25, Mark 15:40-41, and Matthew 27: 55-56 and make a list of which women were present at the cross?

• Which women were watching "from afar" and which were at the foot of the cross? Especially study the women listed in John 19:25. Why do you think these women were present with Mary, the mother of Christ?

• What do you think that these women at the cross would have experienced? What do you imagine they felt?

• Who took Jesus's body down from the cross? What did they do with it afterwards?

Scripture references:

Words I looked up:

What I know about them:

Questions I have about them:

Time Line

←—————————————————————————————→

Compare and Contrast

Compare and Contrast

Compare and Contrast

Character Study

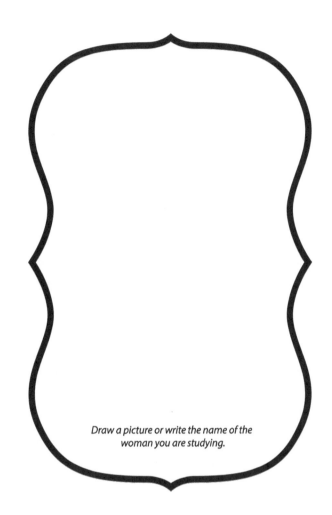

Draw a picture or write the name of the woman you are studying.

Time Line

Story board for:

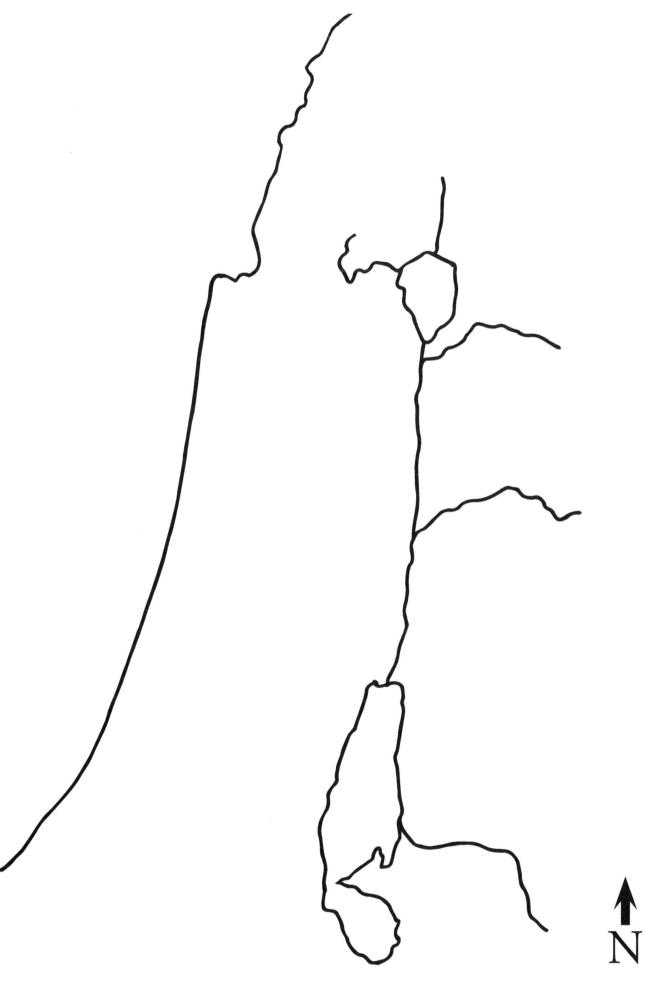

Study Prompts

What do I know about her?

♦ What do I know about this woman?

♦ What do I not know?

♦ What is unique about this woman and her story?

♦ What do I know about her husband, her family and/or her children?

♦ Who else in the scriptures would she have known?

♦ How does she fit into the overall story of the chapter or book of scripture I am studying?

Questions I have about her:

♦ How would her experiences have been different from the men in the story?

♦ How would they have been similar?

♦ How was her life impacted by the culture and time period in which she lived?

♦ Does she (or does she not) exemplify a Christ-like quality?

♦ What type of influence would she have had on those around her?

My thoughts about her:

♦ What would I ask if I could meet her or people who knew her?

♦ How might her experiences be similar to something I can relate to?

♦ What can I learn from her experiences?

Made in United States
Troutdale, OR
05/06/2024

19668607R10073